Other books by Michael Whitt:

LA VENTANA (1975)
SAWS A Book of Aphorisms by A Neighbor (1983)
COHO (1988)
WILD HARVEST Poems from the land (1995)
LOGBOOK OF THE FARALLONES (1998)
NATURAL GRACE ~ GRACIA PLENA (2002)
HAWAII for the dissident traveler (2005)
AFTER 9-11 Land of Moriah (2007)
OPEN RANGE Poems west of the Mississippi (2012)
*OBSERVATIONS Photographs by Barbara Whitt —
Text by Michael Whitt* (2014)
MOURNING CLOAK Poems of love and loss (2018)
BIRDS OF THE MIDDLE SAN PEDRO VALLEY (2020)
STROKE ENSOS (2021)

Hawk on Galvez: A Lament

Michael Whitt

COPYRIGHT 2025 BY MICHAEL WHITT
Cover painting *Hawk on Galvez* by Glen Hughes
All rights reserved
La Ventana Press • mcarterwhitt@gmail.com

Library of Congress
ISBN: 978-1-961884-53-3

Contents

- 7   Dedication
- 8   Foreword
- 15   The Old White Ragtop
- 17   The Drive Home from Houston
- 18   The Wharf
- 20   FORM POEM
- 21   Autopsy of an Alcoholic
- 22   Cloud
- 23   Storm Front
- 24   A Plague of Toads
- 25   Thirty
- 27   Dog Days
- 28   Sunday on Galvez
- 30   On Hearing of Hendrik Verwoerd's Death
- 31   Golden Venus
- 32   Lines on the State of the Union
- 33   Junction City, Missouri
- 36   City Tour
- 38   On Indians and Texians
- 39   Three-runged Ladder of Southern Eloquence
- 42   Good Southern Boys
- 43   US 61 Mississippi
- 44   Transport
- 45   Capitol Hill Congressmen
- 46   We Watch
- 47   Lament
- 50   Hawk on Galvez
- 57   Professor Shot on Campus
- 58   The People's Park March
- 61   View From a Train
- 65   Poem for Uncas: The Shenandoah Valley
- 67   On the Arkansas
- 75   The Dream of Democracy
- 76   Inauguration Day 2021
- 78   The Crystallography of Hope

Alphard

for the artist Glen Edwin Hughes (1937-1978)

> *The Arab name Alphard ..... means
> the Solitary One. Alphard is a red star
> and is located in the heart of the creature.
> It is sometimes called Cor Hydrae.*

A red star low in the south;
it is alone in the dark sky
below the jaws of the lion,
the faint brilliance of the crab.
I still see you on the South Texas
plain somewhere near a crossroads,
lonely bar and all-night service station,
the mythical nowhere we both sought.

There your steady gaze and meticulous
hand record the empty land; a line
of freight cars idle on a siding;
a dust devil dancing across the land.

Or in a dive on the beach at Bolivar Roads
where lost souls sway to music like underwater
plants; a trawler offshore, its nets cast wide.

Before the house on stilts on the West End
of Galvez where we stored our dreams
behind storm shutters; a breakwater
of wrecks to hold back the Gulf of Mexico.

I see you on the coastal plain heading home.

Only in death does memory live:
your slouch and combed-back hair,
your somber face transformed
by your smile into radiance,
as if a light were struck within.
A head-on crash going to Lampasas
to see your mother ended your life.

You are now among the eternal,
a red star Alphard, the Solitary One,
on the wide plain of the night sky.

June 14, 1978

Foreword

This book was written in Galveston, Texas, in the summer of 1966, when I was in medical school. It was two years after my father's sudden death, three years after my tour of duty in the army in Germany, and seventeen years after Germany surrendered to the Allies. Germany was rebuilt, repentant and at peace through the wisdom and support of the Marshall plan, and grateful, not resentful, toward the U.S.

When I returned to my country, its post-war trajectory of "peace and prosperity" after another war in Korea—had now turned downward. It was roiled by protests against yet another war to prevent the spread of communism—this time in Vietnam—and an internal war, the roots of which were in our country's primal division over slavery that, in spite of a bloody civil war, had never been resolved, reconciled, nor atoned for.

The demands through peaceful protest by African Americans for their citizenship to be honored were met with violence by the police and rioting by members of the white population, and the Vietnam War protests were vexed by psychedelics and a sexual free for all. We were at war with ourselves. This book was born of those times.

When I moved from Texas, where I was obsessed with this tumult, to San Francisco for my internship, I put this manuscript aside captivated by the beauty and the birds of California. I wanted to celebrate Nature. I no longer wanted to dwell in my writing on the havoc, which only corrupted my life and practice to no avail. I sought harmony.

I could never quite abandon this book, however. As the years unfolded and I took out the poems from time to time, I began to notice and feel that the sixties had begun a trend toward a showdown, a deeper and wider division in our country that is now disrupting our democracy. My observations at the time, pessimistic as they were, had proved to be prophetic, our government paralyzed by its divisions, our democratic institutions under siege by a populist coup supported by the Republican Party and by some of its heavily armed and possessed self-described "soldiers." Though poetry will sadly never contribute to policy for the preservation of democracy, it will provide lyrics for lament.

Michael Whitt
Inverness
July 2024

Mine eyes have seen the glory of the coming of the Lord;
He is trampling out the vintage where the grapes of wrath are stored;
He hath loosed the fateful lightning of His terrible swift sword:
   His truth is marching on.
Julia Ward Howe

I'll come when you call as the dove
when the corn seeds are scattered.
Sleep now. Dream that this wild land
is yours, that you are shearing oh so
many peaceful sheep; that the harvest
is full in the granaries. But beware
that you do not wake with your feet
caught in the stocks and your hand
nailed to the door. As if it had come
to pass that your sleep were an iniquity.
Rosario Castellanos

# VIEW FROM GALVESTON IN THE SIXTIES

The Old White Ragtop

Voice boxes bruised
by straight whiskey,
hearts beating in weather
of bittersweet memory
inside the dark cabin
of the Bel Air convertible
running over asphalt
polished by the rain,
shining in the headlights.

Dash lights picked out
the jewels in his dad's
Masonic ring, high-
lighted his features
under the wide brim
of his Open Road
Stetson pushed back,
tears sparkling
in the corners of his eyes,
the wipers beating back
and forth wiping
rain from the windshield.

A pain long past,
myth of his dad's youth,
his mother Ada America
dying at forty-five
from overwork, they
said, feeding the men
building the tunnel.

under the hill
for the Louisville
and Nashville line
when he was only six,
and he was boarded out
with kin and only
a change of clothes
until he wore out
his welcome—he knew—
walked to the next place,
running away with the circus
once, mucking stalls and cages,
sleeping in the hay,
now come back to claim
him in a time of despair:
"Texas, Maine or Tennessee
wherever I hang my hat
is Home Sweet Home to me,"
his dad was liable to sing.
But home it had ceased to be
and now no one to take him in.

The white car pulled
to the gravel shoulder;
the father and his son
got out in the rain
and in the faint red glow
of taillights to take a leak,
ducking back into the car
for their last long ride together.

The old white ragtop
fluttered in the night.

Fort Worth-Galveston, 1964

The Drive Home from Houston

Bent over the wheel trying to stay awake,
I watch the segmented white stripe
as it clicks by in my sight and the road
disappears under the car like a tape
that is sucked smoothly into its case.

Through an interchange of highways
the smooth-curving overpass crawls.
The radio's sound throbs in our ear:
music and holiday traffic-toll numbers.
Warning signs on the shoulder materialize
from the darkness and as quickly recede
as pages are turned hurriedly in a book
to find something you know is there.
Dashboard lights multiplied in
the front-door windows of the car.

The flares of oil refineries burn,
consuming the night with roaring light.
A sign advertises a mom-and-pop motel:
FOR THE REST OF YOUR LIFE!

The bridge wades the marsh,
humps its back like a dinosaur
over the dark waters of the bay,
and down its long neck
delivers us to the island's shore,
traversing millions of years.

The Wharf

Sundays down
Industrial Blvd.
I went for the paper
and barbacoa,
the head of a cow
complete with eyes,
which watched us eat.

Semi-trailers unhitched
waited at the line
like colossal sprinters
on their knuckles
for Monday's start.

A switch engine
clicked through switches
thrown by a switchman
in purple trousers
going about business.

Wheels on steel
rails squeaked
like violins
being tuned:
Milwaukee Road
Katy
Wabash
The Route of Phoebe Snow
Burlington
Everywhere West.

A rusting freighter
that discharged
Paso Fino ponies
clattering down
the gangplank
tossing their feet
gaily to the side
and drew a clapping
crowd hugs the wharf.

Lashed to the pier
at the sulfur pits
an Indian freighter
flew a swastika—
ancient religious sign
of auspiciousness.
In the blunt,
cotton-tufted
junky landscape,
the yellow hills
of sulfur emitted a feverish light.

Across the street
from grain elevators
between ware-
house walls,
a naked tree
full of cowbirds
like bindlestiffs.

Galveston, 1968

Form Poem

FROM THE CHART OF A FINE OLD
WOMAN SICK IN THE HOSPITAL

SPOUSE: John Henry Miles
RACE: Colored
OCCUPATION: Logs wood
ADDRESS: Cold Springs, Texas

John Scaly Hospital, UTMB, Galveston, 1967

Autopsy Of An Alcoholic

Two doors swing open on the cadaver:
Cold jaundiced flesh like an old toadstool,
A ring with two hearts joined on a finger
Resting on the surface of the aluminum table.

He lies spread-eagled; the usual Y-shaped
Incision is made and the body is opened,
The intestines tumbling out of the cavity.
Perhaps a woman loved him once and he her.

Wandering the alleys of his wayward heart
Hunting for what once lost is never found
And never forgot, his loneliness at an end.
The burnt smell of bone cut by saw over all.

Some livers of alcoholics are flagrant yellow;
The gallbladder dark green and red the spleen.
A man, Martinez, bore his burden with wine;
All that can be made of his life is this rhyme.

In the morgue's cold bare dark-bright corridors,
Coroner's droning voice dictates cause of death,
Billowing muslin curtains on a summer's day
In the fecund, tumultuous, alligator South.

Cloud:

A one-man shrimper
of the Mosquito Fleet.

Storm Front

A low snow-white cumulus cloud
blossoms on the graphite waters.
Its suddenness startles the crowd.
Under its umbrella lightning tatters.

A freak wind teases the dark sea.
A lifeguard roves in white pith helmet
to call to shore the unwary.
A white ship whitens in the strait.

Sharply stinging the back with sand,
the gusting cold wind reverts to calm.
A few broken beams of sunshine descend,
all that's left of a blue sky and its balm.

Rain hesitates, fills the air
with humidity, and doesn't rain.
Bathers return without a care,
the white ship now hull down.

Toward dark it sprinkles a little;
a little girl in terry cloth shoves
round and round a carousel.
Along Seawall traffic crawls.

On the cement wall was scrawled
in large red letters: LOCO, OKLAHOMA

Galveston

A Plague of Toads

This summer is a time of dried toad skins,
not that or another, lost summer, but this.
Rain clouds roll up like an overturned sea.
In the garden, toads multiply exponentially,
hop randomly beneath green leaves of grass.

Between stonewall and frame house we sit
in a corridor of breeze from the sluggish sea,
our sweaty, toad-bewildered minds at ease.
We live in a sultry clime, a halfway house
between northern lights and equatorial chaos.

A spring wind sheared through the Sea of Sargasso,
and the Gulf's niggling surf is heavy with weed.
This hasn't disturbed the tourist trade much.
It's a summer of dried toad skins in the street.
Tires squash them flat and sun starches them stiff.

Thirty

for Lea

Come alive! You're in the Pepsi generation

I.

Three decades—
a third of a century—
ten years to childhood,
a carrot before the donkey's
mouth, ten to adolescence,
its narcissism unchecked
by acne vulgaris, and ten
to stay afloat in the whirling
vortex of past and future.

II.

We rode our bikes that night,
the arc lamps along Seawall
throwing two shadows
from each of us—
one before, one behind.
The mottled moon smiled.
The waves scuffled below.
We dodged broken glass
and stopped to watch
a Negro man make music
on three lime and orange
fifty-gallon oil drums.

III.

Riding back through a quiet neighborhood,
we heard a voice drift from a dark porch:
"No telling where I could have been today
had I kept at it ...," the past folded neatly
into the future like a jackknife.

Dog Days

for Jim Schroeder

Morning glories are now closed for the night,
the cat's yellow eyes dilated black,
tomato plants and fig trees ebbing green,
the dog a flowing blot on a stained blotter.
Water in ditches and puddles hoards the last light.
He turns away from his darkening backyard—
the leaning flaking fence and sagging garage—
and climbs the steps like a lookout to his post.
Power poles' cross arms like crucifixes,
TV antennae Orthodox crosses,
Lead away in a jumble to a fiery sunset.

It is after a night of heavy drinking
in the bruised light of a hangover
that he wishes for a life of meaning.

Sunday on Galvez

A salver of light rests
on an altar of still water.
Mocking doves, a coronet
of gulls screams and frets
above a wheelchair rider
pushed wildly by a wild youth
across the vacant beach; tall thin
wheels of the monstrance leave
a sinuous path in the deep sand.

A gang of gulls like seraphim loll
beyond the slowly respiring surf.
A crenellated line of driftwood,
beer cans, marooned shells, jellyfish
mark the extent of immersion.
A dog noses the debris.
Gathered like gods, hovering clouds,
ghostly ancestors of Indians that once
lived here, retreat, then vanish
before the emerging Sunday sun.

Censers of mist that swung lightly
are extinguished, fog horns silence.
A stucco resemblance to Sacré-Cœur,
its immaculate dome mingles with shaggy palms.

Priests carried out the conversion to one Manitou:
the Indians worshipped His Son who bled for them.
At "Three Trees" Lafitte slaughtered braves
intent on avenging the kidnap of a squaw.
A father, son and a birdlike one dig the graves.

Pirated from Spanish slavers, Negroes
were auctioned here at a dollar a pound.
In the place of the deracinated red man
the Negro took root and survived an alien ground.
His hosannas resound in ramshackle church houses.

Near the wharf in a dingy room
smelling of fish and whiskey,
a white sailor rubs beard stubble
against a smooth black cheek,
whispers into the whorl of her ear.
Between her heaving breasts
falls his medal of St. Christopher.

On the channel at Bolivar Roads,
a rusty freighter, shade
of a slaver, moves to sea
on a bitter road of light.

On Hearing of Hendrik Werwoerd's Death

The rows of hatred have been sown:
the lines in the sand already drawn,
the harvest corpses, bits of flesh and bone.

Get ready for another cleansing bath.
Can you dismiss it with a nervous laugh?
Draft in your mind a fitting epitaph?

You citizen, wait until too late,
then add your curse to that of fate.
From here on blood's the going rate.

Golden Venus

Smooth blond road,
New York to Texas
to a leading lady in LA,
her mythic arms
embracing the country.

Billboards shout beauty,
motels wink neon love,
light a Pall Mall,
have your dream girl.

America, America,
lovesick America,
could you imagine
your depilated queens
dark headed and warm?

Lines on the State of the Union

The gulf gray as metal
office furniture
falls with its small beat
typewritten on the beach.

Mexican stone masons
smooth mortar between
stones, sculpt away leftover,
banging the trowel clean.

Plate of sycamore leaf
rusts in the wet street:
piratical autumn lays
hold of summer's hoard.

A Negro, cap awry
(skewed by history's dint),
reads the classifieds—
mind out the slavers' hold

into a ghetto's mold.
Our time lurks in discontent,
skin's color: anger's grip,
blood-inked newsprint.

Winter is in the air.

Galveston, 1965

Junction City, Missouri

Behind the bus-stop cafe
        an old man in suspenders
picks out a shiny tin can
        from around a garbage dump.

Walking over to me he says,
        I like to chew my tobacco.
Ain't been chewing it long.
        He smiles when I ask how long.
Oh, 'bout 70 years, can't hardly stop.

The wire rims of his eye
        glasses are bent parallel
to the cant of his cracked face.
        The corners of his mouth
bleed tobacco. He spits in the can.

Where you headin' for?
        Houston I tell him
and ask him the same.
        Walnut Ridge, Arkansas.
I got a farm there, he says.

You know where the Richard's
        Tabenickel is in Houston?
They healed my wife of TB.
        I sent $100 for a window.
You had a choice, I took a window.
        I sent other offerings, it was
worth a million dollars to me
        to get her cured of TB.

And when I took her there
        I didn't have a bit of faith
in the world they could help her.

I mutter something or other
        as we stand on the gravel area
waiting for the southbound bus.
        He stares out at the Ozarks
as though the land could witness
        the truth of what he says.

She died of Bright's disease.
        I lost another wife to asthma
and my last one to childbirth.
        I've had three of 'em,
all younger'n me. You can never
        tell who'll live the longest.

I was fifty-five when I married
        my second one. She was twenty-two.
It don't make a bit a difference in the world.
        I can see there is no stopping him now.

My first wife was eight when I first saw her.
        I was head sawyer at the mill workin'
for her daddy. I married her when she was eighteen.
        Some folks raised Cain about it.

Then I got too old to work
        in the sawmill. I still work
sometimes from three-thirty
        in the morning till ten, eleven at night.

*I've got five hands and I
　　　work harder'n any of them.
They go out and fiddle around,
　　　but you can't get 'em to work.*

They're tired too come evenin'.
　　　Laughing at the sight of them,
he hunches his shoulders, shuffles
　　　a few steps as though
he were about to fall from fatigue.
　　　*Young men too.
I'm just as good as I ever was,
　　　but tomorrow I may not be.*

*I got fourteen children
　　　and forty-four grandchildren.
I been to a family reunion
　　　up in Illinois. We had a big
time. I'm on my way back home.*

Turning a corner into sight,
　　　the Greyhound bus rolls to a stop,
the brakes sighing as they are released,
　　　and the driver cranks open the door
without moving from his seat.

Near where he gets off, a sign asked
　　　Where will you spend Eternity?

When the bus swings into the Houston
　　　terminal, and I begin reaching
for my shoes, his stained can rolls
　　　across the aisle against my hand.

Mid-sixties

City Tour

Who is going to say what order of transcendency might not follow from a philosophy which, to the timeless question of metaphysics, 'What's being?' replies: 'Search for it in human existence... the only door to Being lies in the venture of man's existence—man's being in the world and man's being in time.'
                        Juan de Mairena / Antonio Machado

The Statue of Liberty on her pedestal....
Square, red, brick-walled factories
And incinerators on the Jersey plain.
A black steel arch hunched o'er Kill Van Kull.
A radio tower probes the sky like a pick.

Puddles of gold slosh in the bay's water
The Staten Island Ferry plows through.
Gulls dirty their breasts in New York's harbor.
Wall Street buildings shove like a subway crowd
shoving together at the butt of Manhattan.

People course sidewalks like flood waters.
Lost souls eddy, pool and die in the Bowery.
Alone in the midtown sky, the Empire State Building
Thrusts awkwardly up like the erection
of a small-town salesman away from home.

The Brooklyn Bridge dedicated to the builder's wife.
(Behind every great act, a woman's sacrifice.)
Towering stone, Gothic-cathedral arches, harp
strung with steel cable, hymn of traffic suspended
over the East River's silent flow from Hell Gate.

Salesman, banker, broker, barker, conman
hand in hand encircle the bronze feet of Liberty;
housewife, mother, mistress, secretary, showgirl
curtsy. Kick up your heels, parade, and put on a smile,
in America's musical for the huddled masses.

Honi soit qui mal y pense

New York City, 1966

On Indians and Texians

In a state park, the Texian makes his camp
on Indian ground, so say the signs to visitor.
The "savage" made peace with the environment,
but making peace with the white man surpassed his skill.
Learning English, he still didn't speak the white man's tongue—
where what was said never matched up with what was done.

Sam Houston State Park near Hunstville, Texas

Three-runged Ladder of Southern Eloquence

I.

We are white!
We've gotta right:
White, right, might!
No, no nigger's gonna....
No, no nigger can
take by force that right,
no, not by a damn sight.

Against those black devils,
the race of Ham
without the grace
of God, condemned—
and we aim to uphold the verdict
and you goddamn right,
you fuckin' A we'll use might.

Spite, that's right, call it spite
or no spite, we'll fight
We're Southern by God. And white.
Those heathens of the dark
Will succumb by God to light.

II.

It's not the *Nigra,* if you prefer,
that's causin' all the trouble.
The Southern *Nigras,* satisfied,
I hate to bust your bubble.
It's Northern agitators,
just more carpetbaggers,
shiftless, out-of-work, criminal

element, worthless descendants
of that drunkard Grant—
he and Lincoln started race hatred,
they're responsible for all the bloodshed—
got nothin' better to do than disturb
the peace of the majority in the interests
of the few. The North's worse'n the South,
those hypocrites are all mouth. When they
integrate at home, they might have a right
to pick a bone. I know the Klan raises your ire,
but you've got to fight fire with fire.

III.

All that violence
is so terribly vulgar.
I wish they'd stop it!
The streets aren't safe.

Integration must come,
I suppose,
but those matters
ought to repose
in the courtroom,
not in the streets
run by those beats.

Where's the dignity
in seeking equality
in such a way
respect for law
holds no sway.

I've talked to our maid;
she agrees, I'm afraid,
Martin Luther King
isn't doing the right thing
marching in the streets
and boycotting buses,
which offends the senses.
He should be in the pulpit
preaching patience to his flock,
not raving like some half-wit,
a shepherd all could praise, none mock.

Good Southern Boys

Man, they are real hell raisers
in loafers and old faded blazers.

Married and nearing middle age,
gambling wizard and sports' sage,
though they live in Tennessee,
their heart is down in Mississippi.

Hands studded with their college rings,
it's banter, booze, lounge before the screen.
All the storied grace of the Old South
flows sweetly from the wives' mouth.
The children delivered to the in-laws,
they kick off the best party you ever saw.

They're still citizens of the Old South,
whose traditions, prejudices they still tout.
Any talk of righting wrong they hiss,
cheering on the Rebels of Ole Miss.

US 61 Mississippi

Picked cotton land,
stalk scruff, boll pock
on black earth oozing
winter rain......

Negro shacks pitched
on the white stretch of road.
Dead dogs in the right of way lay,
fetally flexed, legs broken,
tongues squeezed from locked mouths.
The names of the towns
tripped off the tongue:
Hushpuchkena (Hush yo' mouth!)
Alligator (Agitator!)
Nitta Yuma (You'n me brother!)
Russum (Possum)
Onward!

Vicksburg: here
the country changed,
pushed up broken
forested hills held
monuments, statuary, cannon
of the Civil War frozen
in the blood-soaked meadows.
The Mississippi River
from a bluff glimpsed:
beneath the setting sun
a wedge of light
driven through dark woods,
crossed by a black trestle.

Transport

Four pilings—a long cast—
from the rickety pier's
hammer-headed landing:

through field glasses
a dragonfly, barrel
chested, pencil tailed,

hangs low to the water
bristling with minute
explosions of sunlight,

a chopper hovering
low over a rice paddy,
rat-tat-tat—rat-a-tat-tat.

Capitol Hill Congressman

"A moratorium on militarism,"
said the militant old man
whose chin faded into chest,
whose chest reared to belly
and whose belly descended
roundly between skinny legs.

His wattle crawled when he spoke
of a bright peace reflected 'round the world
from the muzzle of our indisputable cannon;
the radiant hope nurtured by an unsurpassed stockpile
of nuclear weapons; an end to the cold war
by allaying any enemy doubt of our moral superiority.

"Might does not make right, but
right and might coupled together"—
here he smiled carnally—
"are indestructible."

"We want power as a silent partner,"
(a lasting fear is what is meant)
pleads the lovable old American gent
in Washington cant, fingering
the pleats in his trousers and
rubbing the slick dome of his wise head.

His bald white legs shown between sock and trouser.
He leaned back in his chair to expound his
redoubtable theory of world peace.

1965

We Watch

Pelicans like ancient craft
skim the tops of the waves
breaking on the beaches
of Galveston Island and land.

In ancient Europe, the pelican
was believed to nurse its young
on its own blood to prevent
starvation or to restore life.

We might call out to them now,
again, when there is more war:
you come to us from the Tertiary,
relic of a world before people,
then cruise Pleistocene ice,
casting a wary eye, you must,
on another hazard of protoplasm,
its brain flickering thought like
an *ignis fatuus*
in an outcast ape.
Oh reveal to us your secret
now in this time of our need,
for we nourish new generations
on the gall of the old, and the old,
on the blood of the young.

Lament

> *For wheresoever the carcase is,*
> *there will the eagles be gathered together.*
>   St. Matthew 24:28

I.

I walk along
the wind-crowded
shore, the brown
waves breaking
on the littered beach.
The gull's lonely wing
slowly beats on the air.

On the horizon
a tiny ship crawls
toward a harbor
like a toy on a pond.
A black skimmer,
wings thrown up,
trolls its mandible
in calm water,
rises, wheels back,
reverses its tack:
a film clip
of a fighter jet
veering suddenly
off course to strafe
a lone fisherman
pulling in his net
flashes in my vision.

II.

Sitting on a breakwater,
surf surging over the rocks,
I hear it singing its song:
"Dissolve the mind
and enter with me."
I watch a small boy
fork up on a stick
the fetid skull of a fish
and wave it in the air,
turning round and round
with its eyeless head.

A lean Negro man,
fists in pressed jeans,
polished shoes, sole
dressing, a gold tooth,
staring out to sea.
What, I wonder
is his stand
on the war? And
death, those teeth
being a gilded lintel
for the eternal worm.
Liberty? Whose?
His people have fought
in two world wars, Korea—
and now in the jungle
of Vietnam—for this country,
and were welcomed home,
not with open arms
but with closed minds,
with fierce enmity,

and at this very moment
are being hosed with hate.
And still they are not free
to vote, eat where they want,
sit and sleep where they please.
And they say, don't they,
that it's the ultimate sacrifice
to offer one's life for country.

    III.

I switch on television,
hearing the commentator
in a bone-dry voice
announce our mission to be
bombing civilians to negotiate,
this official sophistry
punctuated by lethally
bland commercials
for deodorant and mouthwash,
shaving cream to remove
the beard of Pygmalion
that turns women to stone:
smooth faces, stone women,
steel squadrons, weasel words,
while the dead slip into body bags
for the long flight to their home.

1960s

Hawk on Galvez

> *Science cannot solve the ultimate mystery
> of nature and that is because, in the last
> analysis, we ourselves are part of nature
> and therefore part of the mystery that
> we're trying to solve.*
>   Max Planck

I. — Logos

Errant weather
of early spring,
deserted seashore;
black-hooded gulls flying,
laughing in the wind,
wind-blown sand,
gray matter of cloud,
the myth of Mankind
in the back of my mind.

Rising at dawn,
a man and wife walk
along the vacant beach,
sand scuttering between
their feet, the feeble waves
leaving horizon lines at the end
of their run up the beach.
Look how far they reach, she said.
Farther up, small shells and debris.

Water, primordial soup, jolt
of lightning, a spark of life,
chance mutation, evolution...
To what soul fruit or famine?

In history's hand me down, every
culture had an otherworldly presence
to confer blessings, absorb loss.
What better bonds men
than service to a supreme being—
and a common enemy?
Is it the bond that secures a culture,
one that highjacks human nature,
or because they didn't know better?

Are we in God's image
or in his mirror image?
Or is he merely in ours?
Is God no more than a mirage?
She bends to pick up a shell.
The snail wears its skeleton
like armor outside its skin,
which survives in collections,
on shelves, in specimen cases:
an urn to bury time in.

Mind is turned as winter land
by a plowshare is turned.

The heavenly bodies bequeath
to us an idea of eternal order:
like Lucifer we are its fallen star.

In the beginning was the word;
in the end, incoherent mumbling.
Life evolves without design,
though we sing of it as divine.
It obeys laws of physics and chemistry,
which few know and fewer still believe.

Knowledge from a cool white stone
that philosophers fondle; thoughts
lunging across tortured gyruses
and glacial crevasses like mountaineers
or outlaws. Does the cerebral fire of
self-awareness like the earth's molten core
burn below the crust of speech and custom,
erupting into murder and into love,
which accrue the myths and prophesies
where our histories began their warped journeys?

Ultimate reality, both inner and outer,
wears a suit of funeral black, tails and top hat.

Complementarity
of matter and spirit,
of body and mind:
neither one nor the other
or quite one together.

In the beginning was a word.
In the end a disjunction of words,
an incarnation bloody and unhoused,
a day of the seventh angel,
when God's mystery shall upend.

Delicate cochlea of shell
or notched and rough as
an oyster's. Raucous gull
hungrily hunting a wave.
Rare human chemistry
of consciousness, how
can it be? I sit and stare:
without God a miracle.

Death, arbiter of life, of peace a promise,
doth part one from pain, grievance,
is of beauty brief or "eternal" guarantor.
What death bestows must be settled for,
while life may be gulled for favor.

The afterlife limns each tiny life like the faintest of halos
for those who have reasons to believe it real—
it has existed in the human mind
in some form from the beginning of time—
they find proof in holy books and in their zeal.

Can hearts beat for quarks?
Human voices rise into hallelujahs
for black holes, for galaxies?

    II. — Corpus

Embracing in the water
and gratified, the couple part.
Running in with the wave holding
hands before the tide starts out,
they turn to look back at the surf.
The smooth folds of the little waves,
murky with sand, curl as they break.

Drying off, they spread towels.
The sun begins to burn away
the cloud cover and warm them.
They have no children, only
a dog and themselves to mind.
A gull dips and rises suddenly,
at a right angle to the wind.
Is this all there is to life, she asked.

The old house thrust
its peeling chin against
the querulous wind,
unblinking seaward stared
from shutterless windows.
In the letterbox, correspondence from afar.
The sun and cloud a faded photograph
cut and framed behind smudged panes,
a cat stretched on the linoleum.
On a table a button, an inkhorn,
a hammer with a broken claw, books
and a Mexican dish on which
a pyramid of yellow-green limes stood.

Galveston Island, 1966-2022

BERKELEY

Professor Shot On Campus

At the butt of Telegraph
a tall man crosses from campus.
One corner of his mouth is drawn
down in a perpetual grimace by
the shiny scars of skin grafts.

His graying hair in tufts shrouds
parts of his scalp like a moth eaten
tapestry covering an old wall.

As for the assailant who assaulted
the English professor
in the inner sanctum of his office
to eradicate communism,
what is it possible to say of him?

The act of attempted murder
is bare, the barrel carbon blue
of the double-barreled shotgun:
madness acting out fantasies
of sanity, crazy or not.

He looks at the headlines
on the news rack chained
to a pole, stooping at the knees
to read what he already knows.

Berkeley

The People's Park March

The Guard with fixed bayonets
and automatic rifles on tripods,
flowers sprouting from the muzzles.
An English professor
in new white sneakers
and a backpack
joining the march,
a beard grown over
his perpetual grimace from a gunshot
wound delivered to his face
in his campus office
by an anti-communist
nut auditing his class.
Firehoses for drinking
and cooling the marchers!
A pimpled young man
in tee shirt, long overcoat
drifting like smoke.
Rock band Lazarus
on a flatbed truck
with a big blonde
with plaited pigtails
and gold-rimmed glasses
dancing naked waist up,
her big breasts and pink nipples
bobbing and rolling
to the heavy beat of the music,
a frenzy around the truck.

A Berkeley woman in a visor,
with hoarse voice shouting,
with her a man in a beret.
Concertina wire on Telegraph.
A small man, thin beard,
shirtless, shouted out:
What the fuck is this,
a Sunday walk? A man
died for this. (He was
killed by a stray bullet,
watching from a rooftop.)
His lady friend laughed,
putting finger to lips.
A police car was bedecked
with flowers like a hearse.

At the park, a cyclone fence,
jungle gyms, carousels
mingled with pup tents.
The Guard at parade rest
with fixed bayonets
lined up behind the fence,
erected at three-thirty a.m.
by Gov. Reagan's order
(propelling him, they say,
all the way to the Oval Office),
and the beat goes on and on....

Deputies on rooftops
with rifles at the ready.
A block away frat boys
passing a Frisbee, a banner
announcing a big party.
And at Insurrection City,
accompanied by the order
to disperse, the song
"Revolution" boomed over
and over like a broken record.

Cooling our feet in Ludwig's Fountain—
named for the dog that frolicked there—
we watched swallows going to and from
their nests in the eaves of Wheeler Hall,
towhees eating ice cream dropped on the sidewalk.

Berkeley, May 30, 1969

View from a Train

Swaying slowly
        in the gathering dusk
past the still files
        of empty box cars
the Valley Daylight
        enters Our Lady
of Los Angeles.

"Look at that!"
        "I haven't seen
that in a while."
        An old man in a battered
straw hat, legs crossed,
        elbow on knee,
smoking a butt
        and drinking from a tin can
by a fire near the tracks
        in the midst of garbage.
Behind a fence beyond
        a lighted playground full
of children running on the
        green of everyone's dream
of childhood.

Past in place the hobo jungle
        before in time the gorgeous green
of childhood, the far point
        where the rails converge
and the dark summons,
        where the old coyote
limps toward its hole
        and the owl harvests the mouse
and the cactus guards the secret,
        here where the owl

cast a pellet, the knot
        of small bones, fur and teeth
on the desert floor among the spines
        and the snake's breath.

In this medicine bag behold
        the spark that ignites the world:
the red rocks turning to fire,
        the palms and squalor of LA,
the ardor of lights and motors
        feed the flames.

The cities and forests, filth and ice
        burn and leave this planet
smooth and pulsing like the soft
        skull of the newborn.

1975

VIRGINIA

Poem for Uncas: The Shenandoah Valley

Walking back from your law office on the campus
of Washington and Lee, we went to Lee's sarcophagus,
or rather we saw what was to have been his tomb
with his marble likeness on top and a docent nearby.
Look at the veins in his hand, he said reverentially.

There was a portrait of Washington, his hand stuck
in his coat like Napoleon, a pose I had not seen before.
Though it was Washington, not Jefferson (who was
forever writing and talking, and contradicting himself,
eloquent and evasive, who condemned slavery
and owned slaves), on whose shoulders this republic
rests, and Lincoln's, whose melancholy hung like
his ill-fitting black clothes on his stooped and bony
frame, as he bent over dispatches of death and dying,
and whose strong will bound up the Union like a hoop
of steel the staves of the barrel. And Lee, so noble
a traitor, bound up the South's wounds and brought it
crippled but defiant back into the Union, without guilt
for its treason. Did he ever kneel and beg Christ's
forgiveness for his transgressions? Weep for the dead?

Looking over the dense forests of hardwood where the leaves
were turning, we saw above the valley of the Shenandoah
birds of prey flying south to winter, migrating over cities
and farmlands, factories and freeways where Stonewall Jackson
and Phil Sheridan once campaigned, "trampling out the vintage
where the grapes of wrath are stored," a vintage still quaffed
by the waning parties, and we have seen only the Lord's gore.

Lexington, Virginia

BACK HOME

On the Arkansas

for Steve Hill

    I.

I heard a red bird
calling from the woods
along the river.

I saw a coal barge
pushed by a tugboat
steadily downstream,

a pedestrian
"friendship" bridge,
reaching out over

the sluggish river
to North Little Rock,
where the Black folks lived.

River gulls flew back
and forth, dropping down
now and then to feed.

    II.

In the dining room
of the old hotel
downtown where we stayed,

with a sweet Southern
accent a woman
spoke of her mother,

who had a neighbor
she gave water to.
When he backed Faubus,

she went in the dark
and shut off his flow,
saying, *How could he?*

    III.

At the museum
for integration
of Central High School

they broadcast non-stop
angry racists' taunts
hurled at Black children,

the ugliness of
the human mouth gaped
wide, screaming teeth bared

like an animal
at poor Black children
on their way to school.

School was letting out—
I panicked: was it
happening again?

A few Black students
with the white ranger
smiled at me and spoke.

IV.

Our old house with green
shutters looked the same;
I took a picture

to prove to my wife,
my children, and me
that I once lived here.

It was like a dream:
the old Broadway Bridge,
the state capitol,

where nine bronzed children,
who weren't there before,
now struggled up the hill,

the Catholic college
where we caught crawdads
with bacon and string.

     V.

We took the two-lane
out to Galloway
to a cypress lake

where a friend grew up
on a plantation,
the Greek revival

house now shuttered tight,
a chain-link fence to
keep vandals away.

We set our trotlines
with an old lantern
after darkness fell,

tying them around
stubs of cypress knees.
On the bedroom wall

was a poem to
Nathan B. Forrest's
war horse King Philip.

Forrest, a founder
of the Klan, denied
he had lynched Negroes.

I heard the red bird
calling from the woods
on the Arkansas.

Was it calling *me*?
No, it couldn't be.
Why did I return?

Capitol Hotel, Little Rock, February 2012

> *Orval Faubus was governor of Arkansas in 1957*
> *and strongly resisted the integration of Little Rock High School,*
> *which required the presence of federal troops—the high school I*
> *would have attended had I remained in Little Rock.*

72

PRESENT

The Dream of Democracy

We have come only to sleep,
We have come only to dream.
It is not true; it is not true
That we have come to live on earth.
                Nahua poem

We dreamed of utopian democracy,
where all were free, all were equal
under the law, and all vote
on how to govern our country.

Our dream turned to nightmare
from which we cannot awaken;
while we slept and dreamed
our dream was quietly taken,

our democracy used to subvert
our equality and right to vote;
now there's only one woman,
a tenacious Jewish Justice,

left standing between us
and the long-drawn helplessness
of a stacked court of last resort,
while we flail and turn and toss.

Inauguration Day 2021

The wind roared through the forest;
the field is full of firsts,
truth peeking from hiding,
lying for the moment subsided.

Yelling, political discourse
has grown inaudibly hoarse.
Zombies stalk our streets
demonized by tweets,

carry AK-47s,
assured they'll go to heaven;
while we stand idly by,
guilty of our own lie.

As in bed I lay
on Inauguration Day
what else but hope and pray
is there to do on such a day

when reason can't convince,
nor any amount of evidence,
an armed lawless believer
does what makes no sense.

We can but hoard our thoughts,
dream of battles not fought,
for a time to come,
and we speak one tongue:

speak from one grieving heart,
make from hate that new start
that has eluded our nation
from the time of its creation.

Crystallography of Hope

i had to get up before 7
for a doctor's appt. i hate
to get up early, but never
have i been disappointed
at having done so, never.
it was overcast and dull
as it usually is in August,
but the sky so low seemed
to know and held me close.

the reservoir nearly full
but deceptively so as if
to hide from us the drought,
and the fog crept over the road
as if it were advancing on me, a fine
mist coating the windshield
and blurring my vision. lowering
the fire danger i reassured myself,
lowering the quotient of fear, and
climbing Rocky Hill beyond 4 Corners
i saw the sun, its borders diffused by fog
all around so that you might look at it
as if it were the moon, its capsule
dissolving into the morning's brilliance
and with it the contagion, the war
in Ukraine and climate change coming
on us faster than even experts feared
with drought, flooding, and hurricane
and our civil society riven by lies,
of a low forehead and his evil eyes

and the almost—almost—total
universal misery that has been wrought
on our planet, which can still break
into a beautiful and tranquil day
if we turn away and live while we may,
and if voting fails we can always pray
and the lead weight of despair will dissolve
and from the crystallizing of its atoms
hope, a tiny gem in the making,
gleams in the hard rock of reality.

2022

Acknowledgments

I want to thank Carrie Chase for spending many hours helping me with my visual problems and putting a long-neglected manuscript into shape for a first draft. I next want to thank Matt Gallagher for taking that draft and designing the book and cover to prepare for its publication. Without his expertise and enthusiasm, the project would have run aground. Gene Ptak joined Matt in promoting the book with his KWMR radio show *Poetry Now!* and providing us with good food. The last piece in the puzzle was Shook, a poet, translator, editor and organizer engaged by Matt and Gene, whose enthusiasm for the book helped convince him to take it on.

The Nahua poem that serves as epigraph to *The Dream of Democracy* (p. 75) comes from Irene Nicholson's *A Guide to Mexican Poetry Ancient and Modern* (Mexico: Editorial Minutiae Mexicana, 1968).

I also want to thank Tom and Arden Wood, who read the early draft and suggested this book's subtitle, which reflects the mood and content of the book.

Dr. Wes Sokolosky made the first attempt to find a publisher and, though it failed, gave momentum to my decision to persevere.

And it is to Glen Hughes, my friend from Houston, a painter, who first encouraged me and recorded me reading poems to the blues. Glen died many years ago.

It's been a long slog.

Michael Whitt
Inverness, 2025

Colophon

The book was composed in InDesign and the typeface for the text is Minion Pro. Design, layout and photographic reproduction by Matt Gallagher, of Inverness Park, in the winter of 2024.

www.ingramcontent.com/pod-product-compliance
Lightning Source LLC
Chambersburg PA
CBHW020241010526
44107CB00039B/1461/J